It's a Yorkie Life
Pumpkin Carving Stencils
For the Love of Yorkshire Terriers

ISBN-13: 978-0692513507
ISBN-10: 0692513507

Love all dogs, not just your Yorkie? Be sure to get the

It's a Rescue Dog Life Pumpkin Carving Stencils

available from Amazon

DEDICATION

To all Yorkie lovers, big and small.
And to the Yorkies that inspired it all: Mickey and Chloe,
and their best friends: Ezra and Jack.

CONTENTS

PUMPKIN CARVING INSTRUCTIONS

Carving pumpkins are quite easy if you get the necessary tools for it. If you really wish to carve an amazing-looking pumpkin, then do yourself a favor and get a Pumpkin Carving Kit really cheap at your local stores or through online retail websites, like these available from Amazon: www.itsayorkielife.com/pumpkin.

Step 1

Find a suitable table for your pumpkin to sit on. A good table should be very stable and have enough space for the pumpkin and your tools. Cover the table's surface with newspapers, then set the pumpkin down on it. Choose the largest carving saw that you have and carefully cut in a hole at the top, where the stem lies. Be sure to cut it at an angle toward the center of the pumpkin so that it will create a cradle to hold the lid later. It should be big enough to accommodate your whole hand comfortably. Cut a clean straight bottom on the lid.

Once the hole is made, use a large serving spoon or an ice cream scoop to take out all the pumpkin's innards- that is, the seeds and the guts and make it hollow. You will want to be thorough in this process, and double-check to make sure that none of the stringy and sticky stuff is left in there. Wipe the outside of the pumpkin with a wet paper towel to get rid of the dust and dirt, then use a dry one to remove the water from it.

Step 2

Choose your favorite stencil. Each stencil page contains both the actual pumpkin stencil and smaller image that will show what the final design will look like when your pumpkin is lit from within. You can use these stencils for years to come if you carefully trace them on a fresh sheet of paper. Or, if you prefer, simply remove the stencil you want to carve from the book.

Step 3

Use adhesive tape to stick the pumpkin pattern to the front of your pumpkin. The pumpkin's surface should be dry enough that the tape effectively sticks to it without falling off.

Step 4

This is one of the most tedious part in carving a pumpkin, so make sure to read carefully. You can start to mark the outside of the black areas on the stencil by using a push pin or a "pokey radial tool" that comes along the pumpkin carving kit you have purchased. Please note the image in the small box should NOT be marked. This is just to give you an idea of what the finished pumpkin might look like.

What you are creating is a "connect the dots" line that you can easily follow when carving the pumpkin in Step 5. A good rule of thumb is to mark the outside of the black areas out with the push pins every .5 cm, or one eighth of an inch so that it will be accurate and detailed. You will ultimately be cutting out the black areas, so be sure to completely mark their outlines.

While this process is admittedly boring, it is really important to do it thoroughly so that your pumpkin will look amazing when it's finished! When you're done marking all the edges of the black area with a push pin, you can then take off the paper pattern and remove the tape from your pumpkin.

Take note that the nose and the mouth areas are some of the most difficult patterns that you will face when carving the pumpkin. If you are new to pumpkin carving, it may be a good idea to skip the push pins to a fourth of an inch or every 1 cm so that the cutting will be easier.

Step 5

Now comes the fun part -- cutting out the pattern of your pumpkin! At this point, the poor pumpkin looks like a pin cushion. Select the smallest carving saw from the carving set, and carefully start the cutting process, taking care to follow the dotted pattern. Take all the time that you need and don't rush it at this point. Put on some music to relax and enjoy the process. Pay close attention to the smallest and the most intricate patterns, especially in the nose and the mouth.

Continue cutting until all the black areas of the stencil have been removed.

If you happen to cut through a section by mistake, you can reattach it with straight pins or toothpicks.

Step 6

Once all the black areas of the stencil have been removed, go around each of the cut areas and expand the hole INSIDE the pumpkin by cutting the interior of the pumpkin away so that the light will shine through. You can accomplish that by inserting your cutting tool from the outside of the pumpkin and holding it at an angle while sawing around the hole. Your goal is to keep the cut area on the front of the area tight, but allow a wider area of light in through from inside the pumpkin.

Step 7

Rub all the cut edges of the pumpkin with petroleum jelly to keep it fresh longer.

Step 8

You are almost done! Make your pumpkin presentable by removing the excess parts and cleaning it up. Use a soft scoop and paper towels to clean the innards, then wipe it dry again. Light up your pumpkin using electric lights or candles, then take it outside and display it for all the world to see!

Congratulations, you have created a pumpkin that is unique and shows off your favorite Yorkie.

YORKIE PUMPKIN CARVING STENCILS

Annie & Oliver

Baby

Gracie

Maddie

Rusty

Scout

Toby

IT'S A YORKIE LIFE

It's a Yorkie Life is a community of Yorkie Lovers big and small. We know that a Yorkie life is sweet, fun & full of sass. We wouldn't have it any other way... it's a Yorkie Life for us.

Join us on our
Website: www.itsayorkielife.com,
Facebook http://facebook.com/itsayorkielife,
Instagram: http://instagram.com/itsayorkielife_com
Pinterest, http://pinterest.com/itsayorkielife or
Twitter http://twitter.com/itsayorkielife.